"All of of the books in the *At Home with the Sacraments* series emphasize the significance of the sacraments in family life and offer advice on how to convey the messages to children and even on how to participate in the rituals of the sacraments.

"Parents will want to read these books to refresh their memories on the history of the sacraments and to prepare themselves for the simple yet rigorous questions children ask.

"At times Peg Bowman writes colloquially, like a good friend trading children's tales over a cup of tea. At other times, however, she addresses us quite formally, like a good teacher at the blackboard, making sure her pupils get a firm grasp of sacramental history and theology before they leave the classroom. Whatever her style, her writing is lucid, informative, and, above all, practical and accessible."

Paul Matthew St. Pierre
British Columbia Catholic

"These short and to the point booklets help parents to understand and prepare for parish sacramental programs that involve both them and their children. Each book contains chapters on why such programs are in place, a brief history of the sacrament, a theological reflection, and a note on the celebration of the sacrament. The main purpose of these books is to involve parents with sacramental preparation at home. Excellent reading."

Liturgy Today

"This book and the others in the *At Home with the Sacraments* series, represent a unique form of adult formation for parents to understand the sacraments today and to celebrate them in family settings. While the theology is sound and is presented carefully, the content is written to appeal to busy parents whose prime interest is in their child."

Gwen Costello
Author, *Reconciliation Services for Children*

"When celebration of the sacraments involves the family, parents need all the help they can get. Peg Bowman in her *At Home with the Sacraments* series takes an attitude of having been there. She assists parents with their own understanding of the history, theology, and celebration of the sacraments. She also offers vocabulary and techniques that can be used in presenting these sacraments to children.

"I feel that catechists can be enriched by these books too. The presentations of complex history and theology are clear and readable. Here catechists will find language and insight to present the sacraments to those who are preparing for first reception."

Barbara Gargiulo
Religion Teacher's Journal Columnist

PEG BOWMAN

At Home with the
SACRAMENTS
Baptism

TWENTY-THIRD PUBLICATIONS
BAYARD ⊕ Mystic, CT 06355

Fourth printing 2005

Twenty-Third Publications
A Division of Bayard
P.O. Box 180
Mystic, CT 06355
(860) 437-3012 or (800) 321-0411
www.twentythirdpublications.com

ISBN: 0-89622-478-3
Printed in the U.S.A.

Contents

To Jill and Gwendolyn,
godchildren
united by ties of family and faith

and

to Carolyn,
godchild of the heart
before we can even celebrate in sacrament

Introduction

It is always nice to feel "at home." When something out of the ordinary happens, however, we are sometimes thrown off guard, into unfamiliar territory.

This can easily happen when we participate in programs and celebrations at church. We usually feel at home at Sunday Mass, but when it comes to helping our children prepare to receive one of the sacraments, we often end up feeling uncomfortable and unsure of ourselves.

Most parishes have programs for parents before their children receive baptism, eucharist, reconciliation, or confirmation. Often these programs are mandatory—a child will not be permitted to receive the sacrament unless at least one parent attends. Sometimes these programs take several sessions to complete. Why are such programs so universal in the church today? The primary reason is to help families feel at home with preparing for and celebrating the sacrament.

It is also important for families to feel at home with the sacraments in their homes. The celebration of any sacrament is always meant to be communal. Receiving a sacrament is not just a personal experience between the child and God. It is a family event and a parish event.

This book has been written to help you to feel at home with the baptism of children by understanding its history, meaning, and ritual. It has also been written as a practical guide to help you extend the preparation and liturgical celebration at church into your home through family activities and prayers.

Chapter One

Making Connections

As I was leaving our parish church after Mass one Sunday, I was happy to meet Ray and Diane, a couple whose wedding liturgy I had helped to prepare and at which I had sung two years previously. They greeted me joyously.

"We're pregnant!" Ray fairly exploded with happiness. "We want you to sing at the baby's baptism Mass."

I laughed. "Aren't you getting a little ahead of yourselves?" I teased. Do you have a date set already?"

They admitted that the baby's birth was almost eight months in the future. "But we've signed up for Lamaze classes already and we want to sign up for baptism classes now, too!" said the excited mother-to-be.

Perhaps my friends were a *little* ahead of themselves, but what a delightful attitude they had. Their joy in each other and in their unborn child extended to the whole of their lives, including their spiritual lives. Their joy and enthusiasm also reached out to their family, friends, and the whole parish community. And, in fact, when their daughter Sarah was born eight months later, we were all with them in prayer during a difficult delivery. Sarah's baptism was celebrated several weeks later at a Sunday liturgy, and she was introduced to us all. We welcomed our newest member with open arms and hearts. At the same altar where her parents were married, Sarah became a child of God and a member of our community of faith.

In contrast, George was very angry when I met him on the steps of our parish church. "Father is really out of line!" George said. "He's going to have a lot to answer for—having a child's immortal soul on his conscience!"

It took a few minutes to calm George enough to learn what the trouble was. His daughter had given birth to her first baby, George's first grandson. George had come to speak to our pastor about having the baby baptized, and the pastor had hesitated to make immediate arrangements for the baptism. "He said he won't baptize the child until my daughter gives some indication that she's really a member of the church and that she intends to raise the baby in the faith," said George. "She hasn't gone to church in years, but she wants the baby baptized, and so do I. I don't see why the baby should be punished just because his mother doesn't go to church!"

What is your reaction to this true story? Do you think the pastor was wrong to delay the baptism of George's grandchild? Do you think the baby is being punished because of his mother? What would you say to George?

I was as gentle as I could be as I spoke with him, and I sympathized with his hurt and angry disappointment. But I also had to tell him that the pastor's answer was the answer he would get from many priests today.

"If your daughter doesn't go to church, why does she want the baby baptized?" I asked.

By this time, George was calm enough to think more objectively. He answered reflectively, "Well, now that you mention it, I suspect she wants him baptized because she thinks it's the thing to do, and because she knows her mother and I want him baptized."

"George," I began tentatively, "there have been cases where an infant has been baptized based on the assurance that the grandparents would raise the child in the faith. Do you have an arrangement like that in mind?"

"My daughter would never stand for any interference!" George replied. "What's all this fuss about raising him in the faith? Doesn't anyone care about this baby's soul? Doesn't he need to be baptized to wash original sin away?"

George was correct that freedom from original sin is an aspect of baptism, but there is so much more to it than that. The church community's understanding of baptism has grown broader and deeper in the year's since Vatican Council II. All of us who are members of the church are invited to grow in our personal knowledge and understanding. This is especially important for those of us who are parents, godparents, or parish ministers concerned with the baptism of infants or young children.

A Community Journey

Each time we bring a beloved child of ours to the church to receive baptism we are stepping out on a new journey, a journey of faith. Often this new journey seems to be just one aspect of a much larger "newness," especially when the child we bring is a very young infant. Whether this is a first child or a child joining other siblings, we are already caught up in so much newness—a new life in the household, changes in schedule and routine, physical demands, emotional demands.

It is possible that a child's baptism could get "lost in the shuffle" of everyday life. This book has been written to help you to keep that from happening, to help you to make connections between baptism and your everyday realities.

The connections are not accidental. Baptism's relationship to your child's life and your family's life is intentional on the part of the church. In the stories above, Diane and Ray understood and welcomed these connections. Their experiences of church membership led them to recognize how their baby's birth fit into the larger community picture.

George and his family were making very few connections between their real life and baptism. It did not matter to them whether or not they were part of a parish community or were active in the church. All they wanted was the ceremony they felt was required in order to "wash original sin away."

Such a view of baptism—or of any sacrament, for that matter—reveals a common but unfortunate attitude toward the church. I call this attitude the "catalog mentality." Like some sort of large business or store, the church seems to be handily available when people with this attitude need something. As if paging through a catalog of available products and services, such people approach the church only when necessary. Sacraments are seen as isolated events that come up at required or desired times in families' lives.

You who are reading this book might have approached the church in this way, or might know people who do. Ironically, if we come for baptism only with the idea that it is a required service or product, then we receive far less than is intended. Besides removing original sin, baptism also offers the potential for a rich spiritual life and for active membership in a loving, welcoming community. Besides being washed clean, the baptized person of any age is born again in water and the Holy Spirit. This child of our family also becomes a child of God's family. To simply step in briefly for a short ceremony without any real relationship with the church is clearly far short of the ideal held up for us in this sacrament.

The church is a community, not an enterprise. Every liturgical celebration points this out to us, including the liturgy for baptism. Individual members gathered together determine how well this community dimension is lived from one parish to another, but the ideal is held up for everyone. Each individual's spiritual journey matters to the entire community. Each new member and each loss of a member affects the whole church. Your child, like all who are baptized, will have the power to build up the church in some way or to tear it down. Each person is gifted in ways that can contribute to the life of the whole community.

Baptism is the first of three "sacraments of initiation." The other two are confirmation and eucharist. They will complete the action that is begun in baptism. In three stages marked by these three sacraments, Christians are initiated into full membership in the church. This child whom you are now bringing to the church for baptism will have this spiritual rebirth sealed by the Holy Spirit and will eat and drink the eucharist as spiritual food for life's journey. As a full member of this church, your child will be able to have sins forgiven in the sacrament of reconciliation, to be anointed for healing in times of illness, to be joined with another in holy matrimony. Through baptism, all of our children are called to Christian service and ministry. Clearly, sacraments are part of all of life's journey and baptism marks the beginning of it all.

There is really no such thing as a "private baptism." Certainly there are families who prefer to have their celebration of baptism held outside of Sunday Mass, unwitnessed by the parish community. There are baptisms in emergencies. There are baptisms held quietly by choice or necessity. But even these are not private.

Each baptism is an important event for the entire church. Each new member is another reason to hope in the future. Each person starting on the journey of faith joins us and offers a promise of faithfulness to us as we offer the same promise to them.

For families who are active members of the church, baptism celebrates what they already experience—the prayerful support of all members, the shared journey of faith. When the celebrant turns to the parents at the beginning of the baptismal liturgy and asks "Do you clearly understand what you are undertaking?" such families can answer with confidence because they know they do not have to raise this child in the faith alone. The community is present offering prayer, support, information, instruction, guidance, and love.

Not too long ago a family in a nearby parish learned that their new baby had Down's syndrome, a genetic condition that causes some level of mental retardation, some identifiable physical characteristics and, often, extra health problems. The family was saddened when their pastor suggested that they might want to have this baby baptized in a private ceremony on a Sunday afternoon. Their other three children had been baptized during Mass in the presence of the parish community at very joyful celebrations.

The priest was being sensitive to their feelings about this baby's condition, but he seemed to be forgetting the important community aspect of the celebration of baptism. Far from wanting to hide their baby from the community, this family wisely chose to bring him to the community to ask for their prayerful support. Michael was baptized at Mass in a ceremony just as joyous as those of his siblings. The family knew their parish. They knew they could ask for prayers and understanding. They knew this son with special needs is truly a son of God and of the church. They and their little boy have some tough challenges ahead. As members of this church, they have the right to expect us to be with them in faith and prayer through these challenges.

Our Role

Infant baptisms are wonderful times for renewal of family and personal spiritual life. Whether parents are already active or not, this is a time to get connected to the parish, to become wholehearted members, or to renew membership. It was to this renewal that George's daughter and his whole family were being invited on the occasion of his grandson's birth. They accepted the invitation. His daughter came for some classes about baptism before her baby was baptized. During that time, outreach from parishioners made her feel welcomed as a member of the parish. When her baby was baptized it was a true celebration of faith for her and for her whole family.

Each child draws the attention of the parish to the past and to the future. How are we linked to this family? How have we celebrated with them before? How are we prepared to do our part for this child's religious education and faith development? These are questions for the whole parish, not just for the parents and godparents, the pastor and the director of religious education.

The baby, who is the center of attention, will gain all the benefits of this sacrament only through us—parents, godparents, other family members, and all members of the community. The baby speaks no promises, prays no prayers, nor has any insights about what is happening—but *we* do! On the day of baptism, virtually nothing is asked of the infant, but very much is asked of parents and godparents—and of the entire community.

Notice that I keep mentioning "parents and godparents." There was a time in the fairly recent past when the baptism liturgy focused only on the infant and the godparents. Babies were often brought for baptism so soon after birth that their mothers were not yet recovered enough to be present. All words of the baptism liturgy addressed the infant and the godparents.

Now, of course, the role of the parent is central in the baptism liturgy. Parents are asked what they want from the church for their children. A parent holds the child as anointing and baptism take place. Parents are reminded of their responsibility to raise the child in the faith that is being professed. Godparents stand as signs of the community, as people who will support the parents in their spiritual responsibilities.

You might have learned at one time that parents and godparents make the baptismal promises "for the child" at an infant baptism. They speak aloud because the infant cannot do so. A careful reading of the words of the baptism ceremony, however, reveals that this is not so. The promises are made by the parents and godparents for themselves. The celebrant turns to the parents and godparents and, after reminding them of the obligation to raise the child in the faith, says:

> If your faith makes you ready to accept this responsibility, *renew now the vows of your own baptism.* Reject sin; profess your faith in Christ Jesus. This is the faith of the church. This is the faith in which this child is about to be baptized. (Rite of Baptism for Children, italics added)

The most important connection of all is the connection between our faith and the faith development of this little child. We bring the child for baptism because of our own faith. The future spiritual life of the child depends on our spiritual lives and our imparting of the faith. The church is very clear about this both in its instructions about baptism and in the words of celebration of this sacrament.

Connections in Faith

I have been a godparent twice. On both occasions I mused about magical godmothers in fairy tales who granted wishes and changed pumpkins into carriages. Anyone would welcome the chance to shield a little child from any harm or disappointment and to please her with everything she desired.

But there are no magic gifts we can promise our children. There are just simple sacramental rituals and signs that symbolize our humanity reaching out to God's divinity. We do not have any magic, so our children will just have to take their chances in this church with the rest of us.

We cannot promise our children easy lives. We can only tell them that membership in the church can and no doubt will, provide meaning, challenge, and comfort for them along the way. We cannot promise them riches. We can only tell them that as they grow in understanding of the church, they will know that there is spiritual wealth that is already theirs. We are not able to promise lifelong good health, but we can promise that bread and wine and the oil of gladness will always be there to strengthen and to heal.

We cannot even promise our children that we will always be around when they need us, but it is safe to promise that the church—the community of the faithful—will always be there for them. As they are baptized, we who hold these children and witness this sacrament represent that entire community.

I am connected by family blood to the two little girls who are my godchildren, but through their baptisms I am connected by faith. I feel privileged to be a godparent because of that connection, linking me and them to the heritage of faith that generations of my family have lived.

Every time you and I witness a baptism, whether we have some family connection to the baptized or not, we are connected by the very real ties of our faith. The connections not only lead us with hope into the future, but also reach back to age upon age of faithful people who have gone before us "marked with the sign of faith."

In the next chapter we will look to the past, to our history and traditions, to see what they can tell us about baptism as we celebrate it today.

Chapter Two

History and Tradition

"A sacrament is an outward sign instituted by Christ," the young man announced with a certain amount of pride in his voice. We were having a meeting at our parish with a small group of parents who were bringing their children to be baptized. The man continued, "I'm too young to have studied the Baltimore Catechism, but I remember that one definition from the catechism for some reason. And I know when Christ instituted baptism. He did it when he was baptized by John the Baptist in the Jordan River. Jesus was the first person to be baptized and the church has been baptizing people ever since."

Well, yes and no. This young father had covered a lot of territory in his remarks. A woman in the group raised a provocative question: "If you say Jesus was the first person to be baptized, how do you explain that John was already there by the Jordan baptizing people?"

Sure enough. We looked into the gospels and found clear descriptions in all four of them that John was baptizing people well before Jesus arrived on the scene (Matthew 3:5-6, Mark 1:5, Luke 3:7, and John 1:25-26). Did this mean that

Jesus actually did not institute baptism as the catechism claims that he did? When and where did baptism begin?

Of course, as a Christian sacrament, baptism looks back to the baptism of Jesus as its beginning. On that day, Jesus took an already existing practice and embraced it as a fitting action for himself and his followers. In fact, the practice of ritual washing or bathing was common in that part of the world long before the coming of Christ. Studies of ancient religions of Mesopotamia and Egypt reveal that they practiced ritual washings. In the Hebrew Scriptures the book of Leviticus includes prescriptions for various purification rites practiced among the Jews, and some of these include ritual washings. In the following chapter we will consider the various meanings connected to water and to the actions of washing and of being immersed in water. For purposes of studying history, it is enough to recognize that Jesus—or John, for that matter—did not invent something new when instituting baptism as a sacrament. Both of them used a recognizable ritual that was already at hand.

John the Baptist did ascribe one specific meaning to his baptism—repentance. John preached hellfire and brimstone. He was a powerful, interesting character who attracted quite a following of people who came out into the desert to see him and hear his challenging message. Those who took up his challenge came forward to be baptized. The action was a sign that they were going to change, to reform their lives.

On the day that Jesus arrived at the Jordan river to be baptized, some new elements were added. John recognized Jesus as the Messiah, and Matthew reports that at first John refused to baptize Jesus, saying "I should be baptized by you, yet you come to me!" Jesus replied "Give in for now. We must do this if we would fulfill all of God's demands" (Matthew 3:14-15).

Clearly, repentance was not the key element here. Jesus did not come forward to repent and turn from a life of sin. To underscore that point, the gospel writers report that as Jesus emerged from the water a dove appeared and a voice was heard to say, "This is my beloved Son. My favor rests on him" (Matthew 3:17).

Each evangelist also reports a distinction that John himself makes between his baptism and the baptism that Jesus is now bringing. In Matthew 3:11, John says (italics added): "I baptize you in water for the sake of reform, but the one who will follow me is *more powerful than I*. I am not even fit to carry his sandals. He it is who will baptize you *in the Holy Spirit and fire*."

John himself proclaims that his baptism is only with water and is a ritual that marks a change of heart, a reform. The baptism that Jesus gives is both in water and the Holy Spirit.

John's baptism, however, was already proclaiming the new way that was coming with Christ. John took people down to the river and immersed them in the water. The word *baptism* comes from the Greek word *bapto*, which means "to dip." John did more than wash his penitents, he ritually buried them under the water. John's baptism was a sign that reminded people of two powerful Old Testament stories: the great flood and the Exodus.

The great flood that destroyed sinful humanity spared only the just man Noah and his family. Noah passed through the flood waters in an ark and emerged after the flood to begin life anew. Even today the baptismal liturgy mentions the waters of that flood, showing our connection with that Old Testament story.

The Exodus event is an even more powerful story for Jewish people—those of John the Baptist's time and those living today. The great Jewish Feast of Passover still remembers and celebrates the Exodus. The baptismal connection comes from the part of the story when the Israelites crossed through the Sea of Reeds on dry land. Pharaoh's army in pursuit was drowned in the waters of that sea. The Israelites had escaped from Egypt through the sea to begin their new life, their journey to the Promised Land. These people who had been slaves were now free.

John's baptism and Christ's baptism down to this day link us to these events and remind us that we, too, pass through the waters of baptism into a "new land," into a community of believers called the church. We, too, are now free from slavery to sin, free to live as children of God.

There is no report in any gospel that the apostles were baptized. It is also not clear whether Jesus himself ever baptized anyone. However, it is clear that the earliest Christians believed that Jesus intended baptism to be a practice in this new community of his. John tells the story in his gospel of a meeting between Jesus and the Pharisee Nicodemus during which Jesus says, "I solemnly assure you, no one can enter into God's kingdom without being begotten of water and Spirit" (John 3:5). Matthew ends his gospel, a gospel written to proclaim to a Jewish audience the New Covenant, the Reign of Christ, by describing a very solemn meeting after the resurrection between Jesus and his apostles. At this meeting on a mountain Jesus steps forward and says: "Full authority has been given to me both in heaven and on earth; go, therefore, and make disciples of all the nations. Baptize them in the name 'of the Father, and of the Son, and of the Holy Spirit.' Teach them to carry out everything I have commanded you. And know that I am with you always, until the end of the world" (Matthew 28:18-20).

In a class for parents a new father shook his head and remarked, "How can all of that make any difference to our little baby?"

The answer is, of course, that it doesn't. It makes a difference to the baby's family and to the church community that is welcoming that baby. Remember that when Jesus said to "go and baptize" he did not actually say *whom* to baptize or *when* or *how* to do it. The early Christians had to grow in their understanding of baptism. They had to develop rituals for it and decide the "who," "when," and even the "why."

The Growth of Infant Baptism

The early history of infant baptism is not very clear. There is a story in the Acts of the Apostles about a jailer who was converted by Paul. The jailer led Paul out of prison and asked what he needed to do to be saved. Paul announced the word of God to him and his "whole household," and we are told that all of them were baptized (Acts 16:29-33). Did that household include any infants or children? No one can tell, but that passage and others like it indicate that the practice of infant baptism began very early in Christian history. In fact, as far as we can tell, infant baptism seems to have coexisted with adult baptism from the very beginning of the church.

In the early church, however, the norm was adult conversion and baptism. People seeking church membership went through a process of initiation that took several months or even several years to complete. That process, which grew and evolved and then gradually declined over time, has been restored to the church in recent years. It is now known as the Rite of Christian Initiation of Adults. Now, as in the early centuries, adults seeking baptism go through a step-by-step process of instruction and liturgical rites that leads up to baptism at the Easter Vigil. On that night when the church celebrates most solemnly the death and resurrection of Jesus, these catechumens (candidates for baptism) die to sin and rise to new life in the church by being baptized and confirmed, and by receiving their first eucharist.

While adult baptism was the norm in the early church, infant baptism received more and more emphasis as time went on. There were many complex historical, cultural, social, geographical, and theological reasons for this shift in emphasis, and by the sixth century, adult initiation all but disappeared, except in mission territories, and infant baptism increasingly became the usual way of entering the church.

One of the many reasons for the dramatic rise in infant baptisms was the church's gradually developing understanding of baptism, sin, and forgiveness. The apostolic church believed that baptism forgave sin and was necessary for salvation. As these ideas grew and evolved over centuries, people began to be concerned about their children. At a time when infant and child mortality was high there was real danger that children would die before baptism if baptism was delayed until adulthood. If baptism is necessary for salvation, shouldn't infants be baptized as soon as possible? Why risk waiting?

These questions and concerns helped lead to an increase in infant baptisms. They also led to new problems and questions about baptism and sin in infants. For example, baptism forgives sins, but what kind of sins could a baby commit? For what did a young child need to be forgiven? Deliberations about this question began as early as the third century. A Father of the Church, Cyprian of Carthage, offered an answer: The infant needs forgiveness for the "sin of Adam."

Cyprian based his answer on Scripture and on the tradition of the church. Such passages as Romans 5:12-21 supported his position. In that passage is the statement: "Just as through one man's disobedience all became sinners, so through one man's obedience all shall become just" (Romans 5:19). For another century and more the Fathers discussed just how this happened. It was St. Augustine in the early fifth century who gave us the concept of *original sin*. Augustine described original sin as a spiritual deformity present in the soul from birth. It was transmitted to each person through his or her parents just as physical characteristics are transmitted. Only baptism could remove or correct this deformity, or "wash away" original sin.

People are sometimes surprised to learn that the concept of original sin did not come from Jesus or from the Old Testament. While it is true that the story about Adam and Eve's sin in the Garden of Eden is told in the Book of Genesis, the teaching that this sin itself is passed on to each human soul does not have a scriptural source.

The logic of this teaching also required an explanation of what happened to babies who died before they could be baptized, or, for that matter, what happened to unbaptized people who led good lives. If they had not been baptized they could not be saved since they were born with original sin deforming their souls. But if they had committed no sin of their own would they be punished in hell? Centuries more discussion led to a solution to this "problem." During the Middle Ages the concept of *limbo* emerged. Limbo, it was taught, is a place for good but unbaptized souls to go that is neither heaven nor hell. They are not punished for serious sin, but they cannot be rewarded with heaven since they are still marred by original sin. (This teaching has never been considered a doctrine of the church, but for a long time—and in some places still today—it has been taken quite seriously.)

As the belief spread that no one entered heaven unbaptized, infant baptisms became not only common, but *necessary*. In some places it was even mandated that infants be baptized within a few weeks of birth. It was not uncommon for babies born at home in the morning to be carried to the parish church by their fathers or godparents to be baptized that same afternoon. And church law today stills says that the baptism of infants should not be unduly delayed.

Since everyone of any age who came to be baptized was being forgiven for the same original sin, there was no difference in the words and rituals used for baptisms of adults or infants. Until the reforms of Vatican Council II, the same prayers were said for every baptism no matter what the age of the new Christian. Babies were forgiven for all the sins of their lives and were called upon to reform.

The New Rite

Much has changed in church teaching and practice since the Second Vatican Council in the 1960's. Study and reflection about baptism—and all sacraments—continues to this day. We can expect to see more changes in emphasis and even in practice in the future.

Some reforms led the church back in time to restudy the practices of the early church. We have returned to the scriptural sources to understand baptism today. Once more we remember Noah and the escaping Israelites. Once more we remember that baptism calls us to new life and to membership in a community of believers.

Infant baptism no longer dwells upon sin, but upon the future life of this new Christian as he or she grows up in the church. As we saw in the last chapter, parents are reminded of their responsibilities for the spiritual welfare of this child. Sins are not forgiven, but the reality of sin as part of the human condition is recognized.

As the Rite of Christian Initiation of Adults has been restored, the church has returned to an emphasis on the process of conversion, on the step-by-step nature of gradual initiation into the faith community. This raises questions about baptism for infants and young children. They, too, are only gradually initiated into the church. We baptize them and then we begin their process of instruction. Their first teachers are their parents. The first place of learning is the home. As the process continues they also are brought to the parish church for ongoing formation and education. There are also persons who argue that the church should discontinue infant baptism or at least delay it until early childhood when the child can know more of what is happening and understand more of what is being said.

In fact, in the church today all three practices—baptism, of adults, infants, and children—exist side-by-side, often even within a single parish. Adults who seek baptism enter into a months-long process of instruction and initiation leading to the sacraments of initiation at the Easter Vigil. Families who wish to bring their children into the church and who promise to see to it that their children are raised and instructed in the faith still bring their infants to the baptismal font. Finally, a small but growing number of children who were, for various reasons, not baptized as infants, are entering the church through the Rite of Christian Initiation of Children of Catechetical Age. This rite is part of the Rite of Christian Initiation of Adults. In this rite the children go through a process of instruction and ritual celebrations. They decide for themselves about being baptized and they are welcomed into the church through baptism, confirmation, and first eucharist at one liturgy during the Easter season.

Since the Second Vatican Council the church provides two different sets of prayers and rituals, one for the baptism of adults (including the new rite for children of catechetical age) and a second for the baptism of infants and younger children. No longer are children being called upon to turn away from lives of sin. The Rite of Baptism for Children, promulgated in 1969, is truly a liturgy about children, looking ahead to their futures with hope, turning to their parents to remind them of their responsibilities and to promise them the support of the community in carrying them out.

In every case, the ritual includes water, oil, candlelight, and words of faith and commitment. These elements are rich with meaning. In the chapter ahead we will explore the theology of baptism—what it says about ourselves and God—by looking at these elements.

Chapter Three

Theological Reflections

"I just came here to get my baby baptized, I don't need to know any theology," remarked a young woman to an instructor in a parish class on baptism.

The word "theology" sounds imposing to most people. It can put us off and scare us away from some really important and interesting ideas and information. Theology is one aspect of just about every human activity—when the activity is being done with some thought about its meaning. Theology deals with the faith of individuals, and whether we are aware of it or not, we bring our faith with us into everything we do. Theology simply allows us to express our faith in some way. We ask ourselves, how do my beliefs affect these actions I am taking, these choices I am making? We ask, where is God in this event?

In this chapter we will reflect on the signs, words, and actions used in the sacrament of baptism. What do they say of God? What do they mean for us? What do water and oil say as they are used in baptism? How is God with us in this event, and how are we with God?

Water

When your baby is baptized, water will be used. Perhaps it will be poured on the baby's forehead. Perhaps in your parish baptisms are performed by immersion. In that case, your baby's whole body will be dipped into a basin of water. During adult baptisms in some churches, a large font or pool is used and the persons being baptized are lowered completely under the water, or have large bowls of water poured over them, so that they emerge soaked, drenched in the waters of baptism.

What does water say to us? How has it come to be that water is the principal sign of the sacrament of baptism? Perhaps you will answer that water is very easy to find. It is very common to everyone and so is readily available when it is time for a baptism. All we have to do is turn on a faucet and there is all the water we need. But baptism originated in lands where water was often scarce. Far from being a common element, it was—and still is—a precious resource, a treasure in the eyes of thirsty, dusty people.

These people could never forget that water is a force for life, a source of life. Their cities and towns grew up near some water source—some lake or river or very deep well. No shallow creek would do, for they knew that such bodies of water would dry up when the rains failed to fall. And falling rain was an event. Their prophets and poets knew rain was so precious that they compared the blessings of God to falling rain, as in the book of the prophet Hosea who writes: "God will come to us like the rain, like spring rain that waters the earth" (Hosea 6:3).

The Hebrew Scriptures, the books that Jesus studied and from which he prayed, are filled with reflections about water's power to refresh and to give life. Water is the very first element mentioned in the first creation story in the book of Genesis. In fact, to those people water was so basic that God did not even create it. It was already there with a mighty wind sweeping over it.

Water is an important part of the promise of a better future. In David's twenty-third psalm we read that the Lord is a shepherd who leads the psalmist "beside restful waters" where his soul is refreshed (Psalm 23:2-3). The prophet Isaiah describes the Messiah's deliverance of Israel in images that describe a wonderful new world. In that world "streams will burst forth in the desert, and rivers in the steppe. The burning sands will become pools, and the thirsty ground, springs of water" (Isaiah 35:6-7).

In such a land the people could never forget what we today are being called to remember at last: water is necessary for life. Without water, or with impure water, we will die. And so, this life-giving liquid is the thing chosen for baptism. It is an "outward sign" of the inner reality that the baptized soul has been given new and eternal life.

Paradoxically, we also remember that water can bring death. Floods, rushing rapids, crashing waves, and torrential rains have all destroyed life. These extreme swings between dry land with people thirsting for life-giving water, and flooded land with drenched people seeking escape from water's power, describe well the reality of life in Israel. When it is dry, it is dry, but during the rainy season torrents and dangerous flash floods are common. John the Baptist and Jesus lived in a land where life-giving water could quickly change to death-wielding water.

This image is part of baptism, too. Especially when baptism is performed by immersion, we are graphically reminded that just as Christ died and was buried before he rose from the dead, we are to be "buried" in the waters of baptism, dead to sin, so that we can rise to new life in Christ.

No matter how your child is baptized—by poured water or by immersion—it will be gentle. Images of life and death will not jump out at you as you hold your baby during baptism. These are the hidden, deeper meanings, and they are fully intended by the church. As your baby is baptized the water is a sign of his or her new life, and—hard as it may be to think of this—the water is also about death.

Oil

There are other symbols used during the baptism liturgy as well. Before and after the water is poured, your baby will be anointed with oil. There is no mention that John the Baptist or the apostles used oil in the earliest baptisms, but as the community developed its ritual for performing baptisms they looked back to Jewish rituals and saw the significance of incorporating anointing with oil into the baptism liturgy.

What comes to mind when you think of oil? When I ask this question in classes about baptism, answers range from "motor oil" to "baby oil," "bath oil," and "salad oil." There are a wide range of images that oil brings to mind. Which are intended for the sign of oil in baptism? All of them and more!

Oil was an important part of life in Israel. The oil they used was olive oil extracted by crushing olives with a stone.

This oil lit their lamps, protected their skin from the sun, healed wounds, and was a staple in their diets. People saw oil as a sign of health, prosperity, and well-being. In Psalm 104 the psalmist describes the abundance of God's creation as causing people's "faces to gleam with oil" (Psalm 104:15). In Psalm 133 peace and unity among people is equated with abundant oil: "precious ointment upon the head runs down over the beard, the beard of Aaron, till it runs down upon the collar of his robe" (Psalm 133:2).

People also recognized the importance of oil because it had been used to anoint the priests and kings of Israel. Oil so permeates that it can leave a permanent mark. Therefore, it was seen as a fitting sign to mark someone as sacred, sealed forever as a leader of God's people.

Is all of this part of the church's meaning in using oil at

baptism? It certainly is! During baptism, two kinds of oil are used, the *oil of catechumens* and the *oil of chrism*. Both are composed of olive oil or other plant oil, with chrism having some added perfume. Though they are not very different in composition, they have been blessed by the bishop for two different uses. We can tell what each type of oil signifies by noting what words are said and what parts of the body are touched during each anointing.

In the early part of the baptism liturgy, before the water is poured, your child will be anointed on the breast with the oil of catechumens. It is clear that this first anointing is intended to signify strengthening. We remember the healing, nutritive, and protective qualities of oil when we hear the words spoken just prior to and during this anointing.

Immediately before this first anointing we are all reminded of just how much protection is needed. The priest says a "prayer of exorcism," asking that the child be protected from the power of the devil and strengthened to resist temptation all through life. Then he blesses the baby on the chest with the oil of catechumens saying:

> We anoint you with the oil of salvation in the name of Christ our Savior; may he strengthen you with his power, who lives and reigns for ever and ever. Amen. (Rite of Baptism for Children)

Immediately after the pouring of the water the second anointing takes place. This anointing is for a different purpose. No longer are we praying for strength and protection. This time the oil of chrism is used. This is the same oil that is used during confirmation and at ordinations of deacons, priests, and bishops. This anointing with chrism recalls the anointing of the priests and kings of Israel. Each baptized person is called to share in the kingship and priesthood of

Christ. As the priest anoints your baby on the crown of the head with the oil of chrism he will pray:

> God the Father of our Lord Jesus Christ has freed you from sin, given you a new birth by water and the Holy Spirit, and welcomed you into his holy people. He now anoints you with the chrism of salvation. As Christ was anointed Priest, Prophet, and King, so may you live always as a member of his body, sharing everlasting life. Amen. (Rite of Baptism for Children)

How will this call to leadership be lived out by your child? We have many ways of dreaming. Perhaps this child will be a priest, or will enter religious life as a brother or sister, or serve as a lay minister in the church. Perhaps this child is destined for the equally important and special role of service and leadership that all Christian laity are to bring to the world.

We pray that, above all, this child will be faithful, will choose to continue the journey in the church that begins at baptism. Both anointings hold this hope within them. Spiritually protected and strengthened, marked with the priesthood of Christ, each newly baptized person of any age is ready for life and death in the church.

Do you remember George and his grandson from our first chapter? His daughter Mary Ann came to a baptism class and brought her little son to be baptized. During the class she said with amazement, "I had no idea baptism meant all these things! I thought I was just coming to get original sin washed off my kid's soul."

It is clear that the theology of baptism is so much more than this! Of course there is an element of turning away from sin present in this sacrament, but over the years the church's understanding of baptism has grown. As the Christian community reflected together about Jesus' actions and words and their own experiences of receiving the Holy Spirit (especially the Pentecost event experienced by the apostles), they grew to realize that baptism is far more than a turning from sin.

Baptism marks a new beginning. Remember from the last chapter that Matthew, Mark, and Luke all place the baptism of Jesus at the beginning of his public life. And, like Jesus, the early Christians began their life in the community of believers by being baptized.

Baptism marks a change—from the Old Law to the New, from an old life to a new life. In some cases people actually felt a powerful change as they were seized by the Holy Spirit in whom they had been baptized, and discovered charismatic gifts for healing or prophesying. But even those who did not feel such radical changes knew that baptism had changed them. They were in a new community now. Life based on love was far different than life based on law. In some way, each new member could truly say that he or she had died to an old self in order to put on a new self. They recognized the connection between the death and resurrection of Jesus and their own death to sin and rising to a new kind of life in baptism.

Baptism marks membership. The baptized are joined in faith and love. They become members of a community, a spiritual family that will make demands upon them and will bestow blessings and gifts upon them. One reason that promises are recited aloud during each baptism is to underline this community aspect of the sacrament. The promises pronounced are a form of the creed. In question and answer form they repeat the lines of the profession of faith made by each community at Sunday Mass. They are not only what *I* believe; they are what *we* as a community believe.

Baptism gives new life, and that life is a share in God's own divine life. God, who was willing to become human in the person of Jesus Christ, invites us to share in divine life. The church community gradually grew to know more about the nature of that divine life, to come to a belief that God is a community, a trinity of three Persons—Father, Son, and Holy Spirit.

During baptism water is poured or the person is immersed three times. At the first pouring or immersion, we invoke the Father; at the second, the Son; and at the third, the Holy Spirit. God is virtually poured out onto the child or the child is literally immersed in God. The Father, the Son, and the Holy Spirit now live in this child.

Grace

A word that is often used to refer to this divine life in each baptized person is *grace*. Grace is such a gentle, short, simple word. We also use it to describe a type of appealing, tactful behavior. When we use the word grace to speak of God's life in the soul it is a mysterious and powerful word. It may be gentle and hidden, but grace is a life force. It is power over evil. It causes things to happen, changes to occur.

Your little baby, your young child, sleeping or crying, smiling or frowning during baptism, will be filled with this divine life, will be washed in water that gives new spiritual life, will be marked with the seal of Christ and signed with the sign of his cross in the name of the divine Trinity.

One day cannot hold all these thoughts. One ceremony cannot permit us to reflect enough on everything that is happening, although the one ceremony does contain it all. On baptism day, you will be caught up with how your child looks and is dressed, and how he or she is reacting and feeling. You will focus on many parts of the ritual, of the prayers and actions, but will probably not hear or notice everything. Baptism day celebrates the beginning. Everything that it means will unfold before you in the days and years ahead.

Likewise, everything that *your own* baptism has meant and

now means will unfold before you. We have already seen that parents and godparents are called on during the baptism ceremony to renew their own baptismal promises. It would be difficult to participate in a child's baptism without our thoughts turning at some point to our own. The church wants this to happen and includes words that encourage us to remember that we have been baptized in Christ by water and the Holy Spirit ourselves. Why else would we be here with a child of our own?

Just as we stand holding our children over baptismal fonts today, someone stood holding us, sponsoring us, dreaming dreams for our future, hoping we would stay faithful to the church. Because we have stayed faithful, we are here now with children of our own. The dream lives on. There is hope for the future.

In this and earlier chapters much has already been explained about parts of the baptism liturgy. In the next chapter we will put the pieces together and fill the ceremony out, explaining more of the symbols, words, and gestures used. Baptism is rich with meaning. The more we know about it the more we can enjoy and appreciate each child's baptism day and find deeper meanings in our own baptisms as well.

Chapter Four

Celebrating Baptism

When my niece Stephanie was baptized, I sat with her five-year-old cousin Christopher. Chris was very excited about the whole affair. "Stephanie's going to become a Christian today," he informed me.

There were eight babies baptized in the parish that day, so we could not get seats very close to the front. Chris wriggled up onto his knees so he could see, and he frequently leaned toward me to whisper questions into my ear. This ceremony was clearly interesting to him.

The ceremony began at the doors of the church. When the priest invited the parents and godparents to bring their children forward into the body of the church, Chris whispered, "Is Stephanie a Christian now?"

"Not yet," I whispered.

The priest anointed each baby with oil and again the little boy asked, "Is she a Christian yet?"

"Not yet."

He asked again, and this time I held him close and whispered, "She'll be a Christian when Father pours the water on her forehead."

Stephanie was the sixth baby to be baptized in the ceremony that day. The priest spoke loudly as he poured the water: "Stephanie, I baptize you in the name of the Father and of the Son and of the Holy Spirit!"

Christopher was fairly quivering with excitement. As the priest moved on to the next baby, Chris stopped the action for a few moments as he leaped to his feet, stood on the seat of the pew and shouted, "Hurray! My cousin Stephanie's a Christian now!" Before the priest moved on, he remarked, "Now, there's a young man who really knows how to celebrate."

In earlier chapters we looked at just what it is we are celebrating. Now it is time to think about how we do it. Often parents are very nervous about their child's baptism day. What if the baby cries? What if a diaper gets wet during the ceremony? How will we all look when we are in front of other people saying these prayers and doing these ritual actions? Baptism is not an everyday event. Of course we are going to be a little nervous or anxious.

But, like cousin Christopher, we really are all men and women who know how to celebrate. The church takes its celebrations very seriously, but it is also very flexible about some aspects of liturgical celebration. We have some choices about this baptism ceremony.

Choices

The first choice is about when you will bring your child to be baptized. The day of the week is a given—Sunday. The church celebrates baptisms on Sunday because Sunday is the day Scripture tells us Christ rose from the dead, and the day the Spirit came upon the church. You will need to check at your parish to find out how often baptisms are celebrated. Do you have one Sunday a month you can choose for your child's baptism? Does your parish baptize children during a regular Sunday Mass? During a special Sunday afternoon Mass? Does your parish baptize children in a ceremony outside of Mass? Which way would you prefer?

Often parents tell me that they want to have their child's baptism outside of Mass because they are afraid that the baby will cry and disturb people during Sunday Mass. What they might be forgetting is that the people at Mass might benefit from seeing a child baptized during the eucharistic liturgy. At each baptism everyone present gets the opportunity to renew baptismal promises and to remember many things about being a Christian.

When my niece Gwen was to be baptized, the pastor told my sister-in-law that the parish "didn't do baptisms during Mass." I suggested that Debbie call back and rephrase the question. When asked if the parish *"would* do" Gwen's baptism during Mass, the pastor answered, "Of course!" He and the parish were delighted with the opportunity to welcome a new member during a Sunday liturgy, although they felt that most families would not want to celebrate baptism that way. Our family did want to, and it was a choice that the church clearly allows each family to make within the reasonable abilities of their parish.

Another choice connected with baptism is a choice you have already made. The very first question the priest will ask you as you stand at the door of the church is "What name do you give (or "have you given") your child?" I do not have to tell you how important that question is or how much debate often goes into its answer.

It is possible that you "just knew" what to name your baby and that everyone concerned agreed upon the name, but it is more probable that the child's name has been the topic of a lot of conversations and maybe even some arguments. This name is important to the church as well.

The child's name will be one thing that will mark him or

her as an individual all through life. Parents are aware of this without any reminders from the church, but the naming of the child during the baptism ceremony is important.

Often people name children for individuals who are special to them—family members, friends, famous people. The church encourages us to also keep in mind the spiritual significance of children's names. What holy men or women have had the name you now give your child?

We believe in the communion of saints. We proclaim our belief in the saints each time we recite the creed. We believe that saints live in heaven, able to intercede for us there. We believe that they serve as models for holiness, for living faithful lives as we want to do and want our children to do. During the baptism liturgy there will be a reciting of the litany of saints. Various saints will be called upon to "pray for us" during this recitation. Your child's patron saint will be one of those named during the baptism liturgy.

"But I don't want to name my child after a saint!" exclaimed my friend Diane. "We've already decided to name the baby after our fathers if it's a boy and our mothers if it's a girl."

This is no problem. The church is not trying to take away any other significance a child's name might have, but to add to it the spiritual dimension that there are saints in heaven who were called by the names, or some variations of the names, by which we are called. These saints as "patrons" can be friends for us in heaven.

There is one more choice you get to make concerning the baptism liturgy—deciding who your child's godparents will be. Each child is permitted a godfather and a godmother, although both are not necessary. Ordinarily, at least one godparent is a practicing Catholic.

With the reforms of Vatican Council II, the role of godparent has become far less important than it was in the past. Formerly, the godparent's role during the ceremony was so central that parents could even stay at home. Now, you who are the parents of this child play the primary role. The godparent stands with you as a representative of the Christian community. You are probably going to choose godparents who are close friends or family members, people who will be likely to take a lifelong interest in your child.

The Liturgy of Baptism

Once you have made all these choices the ceremony can begin. It is a ceremony rich with meaning that will give us much to think about. The signs and symbols of the baptism liturgy are so important that even children who were baptized in an emergency because of life-threatening problems at birth are brought to church later for a completion of the rituals that were omitted during the emergency baptism.

The minister of baptism may be either a priest or a deacon, depending upon local custom and upon what ministers are available.

The liturgy begins with a dialogue between celebrant, parents, and godparents. Parents are asked what name they give the child and what they ask of God's church for the child. The parents are asking for baptism, so the minister in turn asks the parents if they accept the responsibility to raise the child in the faith. He also asks the godparents if they are willing to help the parents with this responsibility.

After this dialogue, the minister addresses the child, welcoming him or her in the name of the whole Christian community and claiming the child for Christ. He traces the sign of the cross on the child's forehead and invites parents, godparents, and sometimes other family members to also trace the sign of the cross on the child.

If the baptism is taking place during Mass, it then continues with the Liturgy of the Word. If baptism is outside of

Mass, one or two Scripture readings are read and a short homily may be given. Both within or outside of Mass, this part of the liturgy ends with prayers of the faithful, which include prayers for the child and the family. These prayers conclude with a short litany of saints, calling on Mary, Saint John the Baptist, Saint Joseph, Saints Peter and Paul, and the patron saints of the child to pray for us.

What follows next is the prayer of exorcism (asking that the child be kept free from evil and sin) and the anointing on the breast with the oil of catechumens. It will be a good idea to have your child dressed in something that is easily loosened for this ritual. As the celebrant approaches with this oil, loosen the child's garment in the front so that he can trace the sign of the cross with the oil directly onto the child's skin.

Immediately after this anointing you will be invited to come to the baptismal font. As you stand at the font, you will hear the blessing of the water that will be used to baptize your child. Then the celebrant will turn to parents and godparents and ask you to renew the promises of your own baptism. This renewal takes place as a dialogue in which the celebrant asks if you reject evil and if you believe in the basic tenets of our faith. To each question asked, parents and godparents answer "I do." The renewal of promises ends with the powerful proclamation: "This is our faith. This is the faith of the church. We are proud to profess it, in Christ Jesus our Lord."

At last we reach the moment of baptism. You will hold your child over the baptismal font as the celebrant pours water three times on the forehead, or you will assist him in immersing your child three times. At each pouring or immersion a part of the three-fold baptism formula is said: "I baptize you in the name of the Father, and of the Son, and of the Holy Spirit."

Still at the font, the celebrant now anoints the child on the crown of the head with the oil of chrism, proclaiming that the child has a share in the everlasting life of Christ who was anointed Priest, Prophet, and King.

This anointing is followed by the symbolic clothing of the child in a white garment. Most parishes supply some sort of decorated white bib-like garment or a miniature white stole, which is laid on the child at this time. Some parishes encourage families to decorate the garment themselves using symbols that are especially meaningful to them. Even if the child is already dressed in a white dress or suit, the small decorated cloth is still usually placed on the child as the celebrant prays that the child will bring his or her "Christian dignity unstained into the everlasting life of heaven." Some families even choose to bring their baby to church dressed in ordinary clothing and then change to the white garment at this time in the ceremony.

This robing in white is a rich traditional symbol that stems back to early Christian times. New Christians emerged from the pool of baptism and were dressed from head to toe in white as an outward sign of the inner purity of their souls. The white garment is retained in several other ways beyond baptism: the priest's white alb is the sign of his baptism, white clothes at many first eucharists and weddings also stem from this origin, and, at each Christian funeral the coffin is covered with a white cloth to remind everyone that the departed person was baptized in Christ.

You will notice that the large Easter candle is lit and placed near the baptismal font at your child's baptism. The next ritual reminds us that Christ is our light and that each person is to walk always as a child of the light. Usually the child's father or godfather is the person called upon to light a small candle from the Easter candle. While holding the lit candle, parents and godparents are reminded:

. . .this light is entrusted to you to be kept burning

brightly. This child of yours has been enlightened by
Christ. He (she) is to walk always as a child of the light.
May he (she) keep the flame of faith alive in his (her)
heart. When the Lord comes, may he (she) go out to
meet him with all the saints in the heavenly kingdom.
(Rite of Baptism for Children)

As a final ritual at the font, the minister can choose to say a
prayer while touching the child's ears and mouth. This
prayer asks that the child will soon be able to receive the
word of God and to proclaim the faith.

If baptism takes place during Mass the liturgy continues
with the preparation of the gifts. In that case, the rest of the
baptism rituals take place before the final blessing. If baptism
is celebrated outside of Mass these rituals take place next.
These are very beautiful prayers of blessing for the child's
parent or parents. If one parent is not a member of the church
this blessing is still prayed.

The prayer for the child's mother is:

God the Father, through his Son, the Virgin Mary's
child, has brought joy to all Christian mothers, as they
see the hope of eternal life shine on their children. May
he bless the mother of this child. She now thanks God
for the gift of her child. May she be one with him (her)
in thanking him for ever in heaven, in Christ Jesus our
Lord.

The prayer for the child's father is:

God is the giver of all life, human and divine. May he
bless the father of this child. He and his wife will be the
first teachers of their child in the ways of faith. May they
be also the best of teachers, bearing witness to the faith

by what they say and do, in Christ Jesus our Lord. (Rite of Baptism for Children)

The liturgy ends with a final blessing of all who are present, reminding them of their own baptisms and praying for their fidelity.

Water, oil, candles, white garments, and words of great beauty and power all provide a lot of texture and depth of meaning to the liturgy of baptism. Because there are so many things happening, and so many words said, and because you will be busy with your small guest of honor, it will not be easy to take everything in on your baby's baptism day. You can enrich the experience by taking time to reflect upon the actions and words of the ceremony *now* before it takes place and then again *later* after you have celebrated this special event with your child.

Celebrating At Home

Local, ethnic, and family customs add to this meaning, too. How will you celebrate with your child? What customs from your family or families will you incorporate into your own celebration? It is not just a truism that "little things mean a lot." Everything from the baptismal garment to the kind of food served at dinner after the ceremony can speak to all of you about the importance and loveliness of this day.

Time and time again I meet parents of older children who tell me that they wish they could get their family started praying together. Many people have lost sight of simple family rituals or have even rejected such rituals from their own childhoods only to wish they could have them back again later on. There are young couples who begin a practice of family prayer and shared ritual even before they have children, but such couples are the exception.

Perhaps you are one of those exceptions, but if you are like most people, your opportunity to start some religious practices in your home comes with the baptism of a child. Here are some examples of what I mean:

•The baptism candle is a special reminder that can be used for years to come for family prayer and celebration. Find out if your parish provides a candle that you can take home. If it does not, purchase a decorated candle from any religious goods store or obtain a medium length white taper and decorate it yourself. Many families put the child's name, birth date, and baptism date on the candle. This candle can be lit each year on the child's birthday or on the anniversary of baptism. It can also be lit when the child receives penance and eucharist for the first time and on confirmation day. Several years ago I stood at the coffin of the elderly mother of a friend and saw burning there a short stub of candle—the final piece of this woman's baptism candle first lit over eighty years before! I was told that she had lit it on every birthday and on other special occasions all through her life. She had even carried it as part of her bridal bouquet on her wedding day.

•Your child's baptism dress might be a family treasure already. I have seen dresses four generations old on babies at baptisms. I know a family with a dress worn by all cousins and siblings made from their grandmother's wedding dress. What if your family does not have such an old treasure? Well, someone had to start those traditions years ago, why can't you start one now? The new dress or suit you make or purchase can be worn by each of your children and saved for their children after them. Our family had no such tradition, but with the birth of my first niece and godchild, Jill, I made a small white stole and embroidered on it her name, birth and baptism dates, and several symbols of baptism. Five nieces later there are five such small stoles and clear expectations that I will be around to sew the same for any great nieces or nephews that come along!

•The custom of entering a child's name in the family Bible is simple yet very meaningful. First of all, it is an encouragement to get a nice Bible if you do not have one yet. Check in the front and see if there is a place for registering the names of family members and the dates of births, all sacraments, and deaths. Plan a way to make the writing of additions to this book—new babies or new events—into a little ceremony. A simple prayer and then the solemn and careful writing of the new information is all that is needed, but it speaks to everyone of family ties that reach even into the future. In the past this and pressing flowers were the only reasons Catholic families had Bibles. Now you can also plan to read and pray together from the Bible. It will be another way to start and continue family prayer.

At this baptism you will promise to raise this child in the faith, to help this child keep the light of Christ shining all through life. Getting off to a good start with the very rituals of baptism is a wonderful way to begin to learn together as a family how to do this. Waiting until the child is in kindergarten or first grade to pay attention to these things, to encourage family and personal prayer, to provide family religious experiences, is almost too late. By then, parents can feel more awkward than they may have felt when they began at the birth of their first child.

Most of us are not used to praying out loud. We are shy about doing it in church and maybe even shyer about doing it at home. Rarely do couples repeat their vows very loudly and confidently in church on their wedding days. This is not because they do not mean their vows. It is because they are saying something out loud in church. So, too, on baptism days, we might feel shy and awkward and afraid of making mistakes.

With God there are really no mistakes when we are approaching the church for a sacrament or a blessing. Our best efforts are loved and accepted. So, too, with God, there are really no mistakes when we lead our families in prayer. The only mistake is to fail to do it.

Emergencies

Earlier I mentioned emergency baptism. Much as we hate to think about it, birth has many hazards. A child who is in danger of death at birth can and should be baptized right away. In such an event, anyone is permitted to baptize the child. It is not necessary to find a deacon or a priest. I know women who have baptized their own dying babies right in the delivery room, and fathers who have leaned over nursery cribs to say good-by to a fragile son or daughter while pouring the waters of baptism and sending the child into the arms of God. Doctors and nurses, too, perform emergency baptisms.

An emergency baptism is performed simply by pouring water on the child's head while saying, "I baptize you in the name of the Father, and of the Son, and of the Holy Spirit." If there is time, those present can be called together to say a short prayer and to attend to what is being done. If a priest is present and he has the holy oils with him he may anoint the child and even celebrate confirmation.

Happily, not every child in danger of death actually dies. After the emergency is over, when everyone is safely at home, parents are encouraged to bring the baptized child to church. When the celebrant meets them at the door to begin the ceremony, he asks, "What do you ask of God's church, now that your child has been baptized?"

The parents answer, "We ask that the whole community will know that he (she) has been received into the church."

The entire adapted ceremony is very pastoral and welcoming. For example, the prayer that replaces the original "claiming for Christ," begins "N. the Christian community welcomes you with great joy, now that you have recovered your health."

Each part of the original ceremony is included, with the exception of the pouring of the water. All throughout the ceremony the emergency baptism is mentioned, its validity assured. After the ceremony, the certificate will usually mention both the emergency baptism and the completed rituals at the parish church.

Our faith does not frighten us into thinking that God cannot love and receive a baby into heaven if it is not baptized. Our faith impels us to baptize if we can because *we* need the sign, we need the spiritual link that binds our ill or departed child to our family with the same sign of salvation.

A Sign of Hope

The life of a child—and that includes the eternal life of a child—is a miraculous, wonderful event. No one has to tell you that! What you might not realize is that the church shares your amazement and your joy. As you read and hear the prayers of the baptism liturgy and as you see the beauty of its symbols you can know how important your child is to the church and what a solemn and wonderful occasion this baptism is.

Each birth is a sign of hope for the future, a sign of God's power to renew our world. Each rebirth in the waters of baptism is the church's act of hope for the future. We are the church, and each baptism we perform or witness is a sign of our faith in Christ's power to renew the face of the earth.

Of Related Interest...

Family Prayer for Family Times
Traditions, Celebrations, and Rituals
Kathleen O'Connell Chesto

Emphasizes the importance of establishing and maintaining prayer traditions in the home by offering general guidelines, specific examples, and complete prayer rituals for everyday and special occasions.

144 pages, $9.95 (order M-53)

Prayers, Activities, Celebrations (and more) for Catholic Families
Bridget Mary Meehan

Contains scores of useful ideas for reinforcing Catholic teachings in the home, strengthening faith, values, and family ties, and improving communication. Encourages families to grow in faith.

80 pages, $7.95 (order M-38)

Dolores Curran on Family Prayer
Dolores Curran

Prayers, rituals, and activities—everything that today's Catholic family needs to build a rich and satisfying prayer life including: traditional Catholic prayers, contemporary prayer services and rituals for all occasions. 152 pages, $9.95 (order M-90)

Dear God
Prayers for Families with Children
Kathleen Finley

Helps busy families to celebrate the ordinary as well as the extraordinary events in everyday life like going to school, being in a thunderstorm, and reading together. 88 pages, $7.95 (order M-52)

Available at religious bookstores or from:

TWENTY-THIRD PUBLICATIONS

PO BOX 180 · 185 WILLOW STREET ⊛ MYSTIC, CT 06355 · 1-800-321-0411
FAX: 1-800-572-0788 BAYARD E-MAIL: ttpubs@aol.com

Call for a free catalog